PRAYERS
FOR CHILDREN

Compiled by Caroline Royds

Illustrated by Inga Moore

Doubleday

NEW YORK   LONDON   TORONTO   SYDNEY   AUCKLAND

CONTENTS

prayers for the WORLD

when things go WRONG

prayers for the EVENING

"DEAR GOD" MAKE me a symbol of Thy Holiness. Create within ME AN under-standing heart. IF some soul be seeking Love, Let me reflect Thy Love through my affection.

Please Father, help me not to be so concerned about myself, but about thee. If There be those who are lonely, Let ME Take The hands of These dear ones and turn Their sadness into Hope.

So here hath been dawning
another blue day.
Think, wilt thou let it
slip useless away?

Thomas Carlyle 1795–1881

prayers for the MORNING

Now another day is breaking,
Sleep was sweet but so is waking.
Dear Lord, I promised you last night
Never again to sulk or fight.
Such vows are easier to keep
When a child is sound asleep.
Today, O Lord, for your dear sake,
I'll try to keep them when awake.

Ogden Nash 1902–1971

Dear Father, bless this day,
And bless me too;
Bless me in all I say,
And all I do.

Elfrida Vipont

For all that has been—Thanks!
To all that shall be—Yes!

Dag Hammarskjöld 1905–1961

Lord, thou knowest how busy I must be this day.
If I forget thee, do not thou forget me.

Sir Jacob Astley 1579–1652

All things bright and beautiful,
    All creatures great and small,
All things wise and wonderful,
    The Lord God made them all.

Each little flower that opens,
    Each little bird that sings,
He made their glowing colors,
    He made their tiny wings.

The tall trees in the greenwood,
    The meadows where we play,
The rushes by the water
    We gather every day—

He gave us eyes to see them,
    And lips that we might tell
How great is God Almighty,
    Who has made all things well.

C. F. Alexander   *1818–1895*

May the road rise to meet you.
May the wind be always at your back.
May the sun shine warm upon your face.
May the rains fall softly upon your fields
    until we meet again.
May God hold you in the hollow of his hand.

Gaelic blessing

Most merciful Redeemer,
Friend and Brother,
May I know thee more clearly,
Love thee more dearly,
Follow thee more nearly,
Day by day.

St. Richard of Chichester 1197–1253

All through this day, Lord,
Let me touch the lives of others for good
By the power of your quickening Spirit,
Whether through the word I speak,
The prayer I breathe, or the life I live,
In the name of Jesus Christ.

Mary Sumner   1828–1921   *founder of the Mothers' Union*

God bless all those that I love;
God bless all those that love me;
God bless all those that love those that I love
And all those that love those that love me.

New England sampler

prayers for the
FAMILY

And it came to pass, that, as he was praying
in a certain place, when he ceased, one of his
disciples said unto him, Lord, teach us to pray,
as John also taught his disciples. And he said
unto them, 'When ye pray, say . . .

St. Luke 11

The Lord's Prayer

Our Father, in heaven,
hallowed be your name,
your kingdom come,
your will be done,
on earth, as it is in heaven.
Give us this day our daily bread.
Forgive us our sins
as we forgive those who sin against us.
Lead us not into temptation
but deliver us from evil.
For the kingdom, the power,
and the glory are yours
now and for ever. Amen

The Lord bless you and watch over you,
the Lord make his face shine upon you
and be gracious to you,
the Lord look kindly on you
and give you peace;
My brothers, my sisters, the Lord bless you. Amen

St. Francis of Assisi 1182–1226

For every cup and plateful
God make us truly grateful.

Here a little child I stand
Heaving up my either hand.
Cold as paddocks* though they be,
Here I lift them up to Thee,
For a benison† to fall
On our meat, and on us all.

Robert Herrick   *1591–1674*

*Paddocks—toads
†Benison—blessing

Heavenly Father, bless us,
  And keep us all alive;
There's ten of us to dinner
  And not enough for five.

Thank you for the world so sweet,
Thank you for the food we eat.
Thank you for the birds that sing,
Thank you, God, for everything.

Lord, I sing your praise,
   The whole day through until the night.
   Dad's nets are filled,
   I have helped him.
   We have drawn them in,
   Stamping the rhythm with our feet,
   The muscles tense.
We have sung your praise.
   On the beach, there were our mammies,
   Who bought the blessing out of the nets,
   Out of the nets into their baskets.
   They rushed to the market,
   Returned and bought again.
Lord, what a blessing is the sea
   With fish in plenty.
Lord, that is the story of your grace.
   Nets tear, and we succumb
   Because we cannot hold them.
Lord, with your praise we drop off to sleep.
   Carry us through the night,
   Make us fresh for the morning.
   Hallelujah for the day!
   And blessing for the night!

Ghanaian fisherman's prayer

Dear God, be good to me;
The sea is so wide,
And my boat is so small.

Breton fisherman's prayer

God bless the master of this house,
　　Likewise the mistress too,
And all the little children
　　That round the table go,
And all your kin and kinsmen,
　　That dwell both far and near,
I wish you a merry Christmas
　　And a happy New Year.

Christmas carol

24

Pray for me as I will for thee,
That we may merrily meet in Heaven.

St. Thomas More   1478–1535

O Lord God, in whom we live, and move, and have
our being, open our eyes that we may behold
thy fatherly presence ever about us. Draw our hearts
to thee with the power of thy love.
Teach us in nothing to be anxious; and when we have
done what thou hast given us to do, help us,
O God our Savior, to leave the issue to thy wisdom.
Take from us all doubt and distrust. Lift our
thoughts up to thee, and make us to know that
all things are possible to us, in and through
thy Son our Redeemer. Amen

Brooke Foss Westcott, Bishop of Durham   *1825–1901*

Praise God, from whom all blessings flow;
Praise him, all creatures here below;
Praise him above, ye heavenly host;
Praise Father, Son, and Holy Ghost.

Bishop Thomas Ken   1637–1711

MAGNIFICAT

Tell out, my soul, the greatness of the Lord:
    unnumbered blessings, give my spirit voice;
Tender to me the promise of his word;
    in God my Savior shall my heart rejoice.

Tell out, my soul, the greatness of his name:
    make known his might, the deeds his arm has done;
His mercy sure, from age to age the same;
    his holy name, the Lord, the Mighty One.

Tell out, my soul, the greatness of his might:
    powers and dominions lay their glory by;
Proud hearts and stubborn wills are put to flight,
    the hungry fed, the humble lifted high.

Tell out, my soul, the glories of his word:
    firm is his promise, and his mercy sure.
Tell out, my soul, the greatness of the Lord
    to children's children and for evermore.

Timothy Dudley-Smith b. 1926 based on St. Luke 1: 46–55

O God, make the door of this house wide enough
to receive all who need human love and fellowship;
narrow enough to shut out all envy, pride, and strife.

Bishop Thomas Ken   1637–1711

prayers for the
COMMUNITY

Christ has no body now on earth but yours,
no hands but yours,
no feet but yours.

Yours are the eyes
through which must look out
Christ's compassion on the world.

Yours are the feet with which
He is to go about doing good.

Yours are the hands with which
He is to bless us now.

St. Teresa of Ávila   1515–1582

O God, help us not to despise or oppose what we do
not understand; through Jesus Christ our Lord.

William Penn   1644–1718

From silly devotions
And from sour-faced saints,
Good Lord, deliver us.

St. Teresa of Ávila   1515–1582

The Lord is my shepherd, I shall not want; he makes
me lie down in green pastures. He leads me beside
still waters; he restores my soul. He leads me in paths
of righteousness for his name's sake. Even though
I walk through the valley of the shadow of death,
I fear no evil; for thou art with me; thy rod and
thy staff, they comfort me. Thou preparest a table
before me in the presence of my enemies;
thou anointest my head with oil, my cup overflows.
Surely goodness and mercy shall follow me all the
days of my life; and I shall dwell in the house of the
Lord for ever.

Psalm 23

God be in my head,
And in my understanding;

God be in my eyes,
And in my looking;

God be in my mouth,
And in my speaking;

God be in my heart,
And in my thinking;

God be at my end,
And at my departing.

from the Sarum Missal

Love bade me welcome; yet my soul drew back,
Guilty of dust and sin.
But quick-eyed Love, observing me grow slack
From my first entrance in,
Drew nearer to me, sweetly questioning
If I lack'd anything.

   "A guest," I answer'd, "worthy to be here:"
Love said, "You shall be he."
   "I, the unkind, ungrateful? Ah, my dear,
I cannot look on Thee."
Love took my hand and smiling did reply,
   "Who made the eyes but I?"

   "Truth, Lord, but I have marr'd them: let my shame
Go where it doth deserve."
   "And know you not," says Love, "Who bore the blame?"
   "My dear, then I will serve."
   "You must sit down," says Love, "and taste my meat."
So I did sit and eat.

George Herbert 1593–1633

God bless Africa: guard her children,
guide her rulers, and give her peace.

Trevor Huddleston   b. 1913

prayers for the
WORLD

O most high, almighty, good Lord, God: to you belong
Praise, glory, honor, and all blessing.

Praised be my Lord by all his creatures: and chiefly
by our brother the sun, who brings us the day
and brings us the light. Fair is he, and shines with
a very great splendor: O Lord, he points us to you.

Praised be my Lord by our sister the moon: and by
the stars which you have set clear and lovely in heaven.

Praised be my Lord by our brother the wind:
and by air and cloud, calms and all weather,
by which you uphold life in all creatures.

Praised be my Lord by our sister water: who is very
useful to us and humble and precious and clean.

Praised be my Lord by our brother fire, through whom
you give light in the darkness: and he is bright
and pleasant and very mighty and strong.

Praised be my Lord by our mother the earth,
who sustains us and keeps us: and brings forth fruits
of different kinds, flowers of many colors, and grass.

St. Francis of Assisi   1182–1226

O you gotta get a glory
   In the work you do,
A Hallelujah chorus
   In the heart of you.
Paint or tell a story,
   Sing or shovel coal,
But you gotta get a glory
   Or the job lacks soul.

from a Black spiritual

Go tell it on the mountain.
    Over the hills and everywhere,
Go tell it on the mountain
    That Jesus Christ is born.

from a Black spiritual

I bind unto myself today
    The power of God to hold and lead,
His eye to watch, his might to stay,
    His ear to hearken to my need;
The wisdom of my God to teach,
    His hand to guide, his shield to ward;
The word of God to give me speech,
    His heavenly host to be my guard.

Christ be with me, Christ within me,
Christ behind me, Christ before me,
Christ beside me, Christ to win me,
Christ to comfort and restore me,
Christ beneath me, Christ above me,
Christ in quiet, Christ in danger,
Christ in hearts of all that love me,
Christ in mouth of friend and stranger.

The Breastplate of St. Patrick

Earth is your talent. Use it.

C. Day-Lewis   1904–1972

We are going home to many who cannot read.
So, Lord, make us to be Bibles
so that those who cannot read the Book can read it in us.

Chinese prayer

Dear Father,
    Hear and bless
Your beasts
    And singing birds:
And guard
    With tenderness
Small things
    That have no words.

Glory be to God for dappled things—
For skies of couple-colour as a brinded cow;
For rose-moles all in stipple upon trout that swim;
Fresh-firecoal chestnut-falls; finches' wings;
Landscape plotted and pieced—fold, fallow, and plough;
And all trades, their gear and tackle and trim.

All things counter, original, spare, strange;
Whatever is fickle, freckled (who knows how?)
With swift, slow; sweet, sour; adazzle, dim;
He fathers-forth whose beauty is past change:
Praise him.

Gerard Manley Hopkins 1844–1889

We can do no great things,
Only small things with great love.

Mother Teresa of Calcutta

He prayeth best,
Who loveth best
All things both
Great and small;
For the dear God
Who loveth us,
He made and loveth all.

Samuel Taylor Coleridge   1772–1834

42

Even if it seems inadequate in your eyes,
None of the good you do is ever lost.

when things go
WRONG

Lord, make me an instrument of your peace.
    Where there is hatred, let me sow love;
    Where there is injury, pardon;
    Where there is doubt, faith;
    Where there is despair, hope;
    Where there is darkness, light;
    And where there is sadness, joy.
O divine Master, grant that I may not so much seek
    To be consoled as to console,
    To be understood as to understand,
    To be loved as to love
For it is in giving that we receive;
It is in pardoning that we are pardoned;
And it is in dying that we are born to eternal life.

St. Francis of Assisi 1182–1226

When I despise myself or the world
let me find your image within me again.
Blessed are you, O Lord,
who have made me as you wanted me.

I believe in the sun even when it does not shine.
I believe in love even when I do not feel it.
I believe in God even when He is silent.

Inscription on the walls of a cellar in Cologne, Germany, where Jews hid from the Nazis.

O God,
I try and think about you
but I can't see your face.
I try and talk to you,
but you don't answer me.
How can I know you love me
unless I feel your touch?
And how can I reach out to you
if you have gone away?
I want to understand you,
but you are too hard for me;
so I am waiting here in the dark,
waiting for you, O God.

Janet Morley

As the rain hides the stars,
as the autumn mist hides the hills,
as the clouds veil the blue of the sky,
so the dark happenings of my lot
hide the shining of your face from me.
Yet, if I may hold your hand in the darkness,
it is enough.
Since I know that, though I may stumble in my going,
You do not fall.

Gaelic prayer

I danced in the morning
When the world was begun,
And I danced in the moon
And the stars and the sun,
And I came down from heaven
And danced on the earth;
At Bethlehem
I had my birth:

Dance, then, wherever you may be;
I am the Lord of the Dance, said he,
And I'll lead you all, wherever you may be,
And I'll lead you all in the dance, said he.

I danced on the Sabbath
And I cured the lame:
The holy people
Said it was a shame.
They whipped and they stripped
And they hung me high
And left me there
On a cross to die:

I danced on a Friday
When the sky turned black;
It's hard to dance
With the devil on your back.
They buried my body
And they thought I'd gone;
But I am the dance
And I still go on:

They cut me down
And I leap up high;
I am the life
That'll never, never die;
I'll live in you
If you'll live in me;
I am the Lord
Of the Dance, said he.

Dance, then, wherever you may be;
I am the Lord of the Dance, said he,
And I'll lead you all, wherever you may be,
And I'll lead you all in the dance, said he.

Sydney Carter   b. 1915

We give them back to you, dear Lord,
who gavest them to us.
Yet as thou didst not lose them in giving,
so we have not lost them by their return.
For what is thine is ours always if
we are thine.
And life is eternal and love is immortal,
and death is only a horizon,
and a horizon is nothing more
than the limit of our sight.

Quaker prayer

God give us grace to accept with serenity
the things that cannot be changed, courage to
change the things which should be changed,
and the wisdom to distinguish the one from
the other.

Reinhold Niebuhr   1892–1971

Love is not changed by death—and nothing is lost,
and all in the end is harvest.

Edith Sitwell   1887–1964

Watch, Lord,
with those who wake,
or watch, or weep tonight,
and give your angels
charge over those who sleep.
Tend your sick ones,
O Lord Jesus Christ;
rest your weary ones;
bless your dying ones;
soothe your suffering ones;
pity your afflicted ones;
shield your joyous ones.
And all for your love's sake.

St. Augustine 354–430

O heavenly Father, protect and bless
all things that have breath:
Guard them from all evil
and let them sleep in peace.

Albert Schweitzer   1875–1965

prayers for the
EVENING

Matthew, Mark, Luke, and John,
Bless the bed that I lie on.
Before I lay me down to sleep
I give my soul to Christ to keep.
Four corners to my bed,
Four angels overspread:
One at the head, one at the feet,
And two to guard me while I sleep.
I go by sea, I go by land,
The Lord made me with His right hand,
If any danger come to me,
Sweet Jesus Christ, deliver me.
He is the branch and I'm the flower,
May God send me a happy hour.

Preserve us, O Lord, while waking,
and guard us while sleeping;
that awake we may watch with Christ,
and asleep we may rest in peace.

Lord, be the guest of this house.
Keep far from it all the deceits of the evil one.
May your holy angels watch over us
as guardians of our peace;
and may your blessing be always upon us.

Now I lay me down to sleep,
I pray thee, Lord, thy child to keep;
Thy love to guard me through the night
And wake me in the morning light.

Lord, when I am afraid of sleep and afraid of the
darkness, make me remember that in peace I can lay
me down in sleep, for you alone make me to dwell in
safety, and the darkness is not dark to you.
Lord, help me to put my trust in you when I am afraid. Amen

Now the day is over,
    Night is drawing nigh,
Shadows of the evening
    Steal across the sky.

Now the darkness gathers,
    Stars begin to peep,
Birds and beasts and flowers
    Soon will be asleep.

Jesus, give the weary
    Calm and sweet repose;
With thy tenderest blessing
    May our eyelids close.

Grant to little children
    Visions bright of thee;
Guard the sailors tossing
    On the deep, blue sea.

When the morning wakens,
    Then may I arise
Pure, and fresh, and sinless
    In thy holy eyes.

    S. Baring-Gould 1834–1924

Lighten our darkness, we beseech thee, O Lord;
and by thy great mercy defend us from all perils
and dangers of this night; for the love of thy
only Son, our Saviour, Jesus Christ. Amen.

Book of Common Prayer

Dear Jesus, as a hen covers her chicks with her wings to keep them safe, do you this dark night protect us under your golden wings.

Prayer from India

For permission to reproduce copyright materials, acknowledgment and thanks
are due to the following:

Curtis Brown Ltd. and Andre Deutsch Ltd. for "Now Another Day Is Break-
ing" by Ogden Nash from *I Wouldn't Have Missed It* copyright © 1961, 1962 by
Ogden Nash; Faber and Faber Ltd. for "For All That Has Been—Thanks!" by
Dag Hammarskjöld from *Markings,* translated by W. H. Auden and Leif
Sjoberg; The Mothers' Union for "All Through This Day, Lord" by Mary
Sumner, founder of the Mothers' Union; Victor Gollancz for a short prayer by
Albert Schweitzer from *God of a Hundred Names* compiled by Barbara Greene
and Victor Gollancz; Stainer and Bell Ltd. and Galaxy Music Corporation for
Lord of the Dance by Sydney Carter © Galaxy Music Corporation, Sole U.S.
Agent; Janet Morley for a new prayer; The Rt. Revd. Trevor Huddleston,
C.R., for his short prayer "God Bless Africa."

While every effort has been made to obtain permission, there may still be
cases in which we have failed to trace a copyright holder, and we would like to
apologize for any apparent negligence.